GHOSTS AND POLTERGEISTS

STORIES OF THE SUPERNATURAL

by David West

illustrated by Terry

Rosen Classroom Books & Materials™
New York

Published in 2006 by The Rosen Publishing Group, Inc.
29 East 21st Street, New York, NY 10010

Copyright © 2006 David West Books

First edition, 2006

Designed and produced by
David West Books

Editor: Dominique Crowley

Photo credits:
Page 4 (bottom left) – Max Azison
Page 4 (bottom right) – Teresa Hurst
Page 5 (top right) – Peter Guess, Dreamstime.com
Page 6 – Katherine Garrenson
Page 7 – Image provided by Dreamstime.com
Page 44-45 – Hermann Danzmayr

ISBN: 1-4042-0805-4 (pbk.)
ISBN: 1-4042-6261-X (6 pack)

Manufactured in China

CONTENTS

A GHOSTLY WORLD

Since ancient times, people have believed in the afterlife (life after death) and ghosts. Ancient Egyptians believed that you would need your body in the next life, so they mummified the bodies of the dead to preserve them. Romans believed that the spirits of their ancestors, called larvae, returned as ghosts to haunt the living.

GRAPHIC GHOSTS AND POLTERGEISTS MYSTERIES

CELEBRATIONS

Halloween, on October 31, was traditionally the night ghosts walked the earth. Bonfires were lit to summon the spirits and please them by keeping them warm. On the "Day of the Dead" (November 2) in Mexico, people remember and celebrate those who have died.

Today, Halloween is celebrated with homemade jack-o'-lanterns (above) and children demanding "tricks or treats."

A skeleton dressed in white (above) decorates the front of a shop during the Mexican "Day of the Dead."

FAVORITE HAUNTS

Many people believe that graveyards are the most likely place to see a ghost. According to folklore, however, ghosts haunt the places where they died. When a new graveyard was built in the Dark Ages, pagans sacrificed victims so that their spirits would become the new graveyard's guardians. People have often reported seeing wisps of light in graveyards, believing them to be ghosts. Today, scientists think they are probably luminous gases rising from the rotting corpses.

Haunted houses are far more common places to come across ghosts, especially if a person has been murdered or buried in the house. Both 112 Ocean Avenue, Amityville, New York (see page 22), and Borley Rectory, England, are reportedly the most haunted houses in the world.

Graveyards are actually unlikely haunts for ghosts.

Borley Rectory, in Essex, (below) was the scene of ghostly hauntings of a nun from 1927 until it burnt down in 1939. Upon inspection, bones of a young woman were found under the cellar floor.

WHAT IS A GHOST?

The traditional representation of a ghost as a person under a bedsheet has become more sophisticated as more and more ghost films hit the silver screen and computer-generated special effects improve.

FROM SHAKESPEARE TO HOLLYWOOD
Ghosts have been portrayed in literature from the days of the ancient Greeks. The early Greek poet Homer, c. 750 B.C., described the ghost of Hector in his epic poem the *Iliad*. Early Chinese literature and Roman writings also describe ghosts. Most famously of all, William Shakespeare (1564–1616) wrote plays with ghostly goings-on such as *Hamlet* and *Macbeth*. In *A Christmas Carol* (1843), by Charles Dickens, a miser called Scrooge is visited by three ghosts. Today, cinema has kept the image of ghosts firmly in our minds with classic films such as *Poltergeist* (1982), *Ghostbusters* (1984), *Ghost* (1989), and the remake of *The Amityville Horror* (2005). See page 22 onward for the events on which this latter film is based.

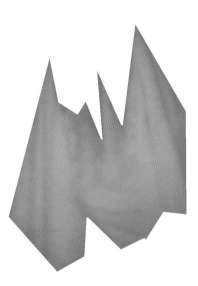

The classic image of a ghost is of a person draped in a white sheet.

TYPES OF GHOSTS

Ghosts or spirits can appear in different forms and have a definite purpose, according to some believers. They might visit people to give warnings, take revenge on those who have hurt them, or request that their bodies be buried properly in order for their spirits to rest in peace. A few of the better known spirits from around the world are described at right.

GETTING IN TOUCH

People called mediums claim to be able to contact the dead. One way of doing this is to gather a group of people around a table and have them holding hands. The medium calls up the spirit of the dead person and acts as an intermediary between the spirit and its living relatives. This is called a séance. It has been claimed that mediums have helped police to catch murderers.

Ouija boards are used to "talk" with the dead. A number of people put their fingers on a small glass, which the spirit then moves to answer questions by spelling out words.

GHOSTLY FORMS

Banshee – *an Irish ghost in the form of a screaming woman. It forewarns a person of his or her time of death.*

Duppy – *a Jamaican evil spirit said to live in the buttress roots of silk cotton trees.*

Ghoul – *an Arabian demon that lives in the desert. It is said to suck the blood of humans.*

Jinnie – *a Middle Eastern spirit made of smokeless fire. A jinnie can be controlled with magic by binding it to an object, such as a lamp, as in the story of Aladdin.*

Poltergeist – *an invisible ghost that is violent, noisy, and can even cause fires. It is believed to be active around teenagers who are troubled.*

Virika – *a small, red, evil spirit from India. A virika will roam about at night making strange gibbering noises.*

LORD DUFFERIN AND THE GHOSTLY WARNING

1880, TULLEMORE, COUNTY WEXFORD, IRELAND. THE ENGLISH LORD DUFFERIN IS STAYING AT THE HOUSE OF A FRIEND.

CLUMP

HURRUMPH!

CLUMP

CLUMP

WHO GOES THERE?

CLUMP

CLUMP

CLUMP

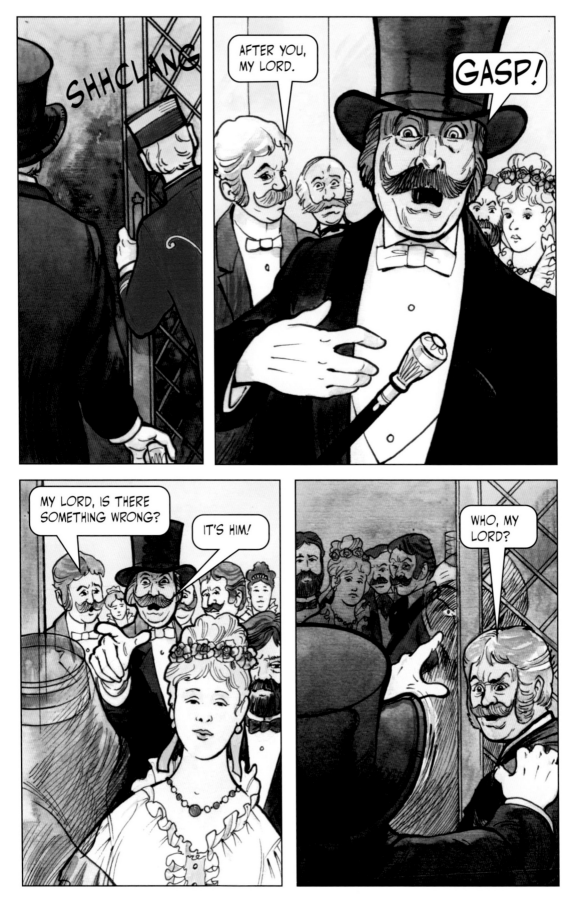

THE MACOMB POLTERGEIST

AUGUST 7, 1948, WILLEY'S FARM, MACOMB, ILLINOIS, USA.

HEY, CAN ANYONE SMELL BURNING?

POP, WHY CAN'T I STAY WITH MOM IN BLOOMINGTON?

MAYBE IT'S THE STOVE.

LISTEN, WANET, WE'VE BEEN THROUGH THIS BEFORE...

WANET, AGE 13, AND HER BROTHER, ARTHUR JUNIOR, 8, ARE LIVING WITH THEIR FATHER, ARTHUR MCNEIL, AFTER THEIR PARENTS' DIVORCE. THEY ARE STAYING WITH THEIR RELATIVES, MR. AND MRS. CHARLES WILLEY.

BUT IT'S SO UNFAIR!

HEAVEN HELP US! THE WOOD BOX IS ON FIRE!

18

THE MCNEILS AND WILLEYS MOVE TO A VACANT HOUSE NEARBY, BUT THE FIRES CONTINUE TO BREAK OUT. MEANWHILE, THE STORY MAKES THE NATIONAL NEWS. ON AUGUST 22, MORE THAN A THOUSAND PEOPLE VISIT WILLEY'S FARM.

I DON'T UNDERSTAND IT. WE'VE HAD EVERYONE FROM THE FIRE DEPARTMENT TO THE AIR FORCE TRYING TO FIND THE REASON FOR THE FIRES. AND THEY'VE COME UP WITH NOTHING.

AUGUST 30

MR. WILLEY, THIS IS THE STATE ATTORNEY, KEITH SCOTT. HE WOULD LIKE TO ASK YOUR FAMILY A FEW QUESTIONS IN AN EFFORT TO FIND THE CAUSE OF THESE FIRES.

SURE THING, FIRE MARSHAL BURGARD.

ALTHOUGH THE STORY DIED DOWN QUICKLY, MOST PEOPLE WERE NOT CONVINCED BY WANET'S CONFESSION. MANY PARANORMAL INVESTIGATORS THINK THE MACOMB FIRES AT THE WILLEYS' FARM WERE THE WORK OF A POLTERGEIST.   **THE END**

THE HAUNTED HOUSE AT AMITYVILLE

FEBRUARY 1976. A REPORTER FROM NEW YORK'S LOCAL TELEVISION STATION, WNEW, IS BROADCASTING LIVE...

WE ARE OUTSIDE 112 OCEAN AVENUE, AMITYVILLE, LONG ISLAND, WHERE A SÉANCE IS BEING HELD BY ED AND LORRAINE WARREN, TWO OF THE MOST FAMOUS EXPERTS IN THE PARANORMAL.

THEY ARE INVESTIGATING CLAIMS BY THE HOMEOWNERS THAT THE HOUSE IS HAUNTED. GEORGE AND KATHY LUTZ, AND THEIR THREE CHILDREN, SAY THEY FLED FOR THEIR LIVES AFTER SPENDING ONLY 28 DAYS HERE.

SOME OF YOU MAY REMEMBER THAT THIS SAME HOUSE WAS RECENTLY THE SCENE OF A GRISLY MURDER.

ONLY 14 MONTHS AGO, RONALD DEFEO JUNIOR MURDERED HIS ENTIRE FAMILY WITH A HIGH-POWERED RIFLE AS THEY SLEPT.

DEFEO CLAIMED THAT, AT THE TIME OF THE SHOOTING, HE HEARD VOICES URGING HIM TO DO IT.

31

34

37

"THERE WERE ALSO STRANGE, SICKLY ODORS WAFTING THROUGH THE HOUSE. THEN KATHY STARTED GETTING TOUCHED BY... WELL, YOU TELL HIM, KATHY."

"IT WAS VERY CREEPY. I WOULD BE DOING SOME HOUSEHOLD CHORES, WHEN SUDDENLY I WOULD FEEL A STRANGE PRESENCE..."

WHA...

"...INVISIBLE HANDS WOULD GRAB ME."

AAAAAHHHH!

"SOMETIMES, I WOULD END UP WITH RED WELTS. ONE NIGHT, IT FELT LIKE I WAS BEING LIFTED UP! IT WAS MORE HORRIFYING FOR GEORGE THAN FOR ME."

YEAH! I WOKE UP TO SEE HER THERE...

40

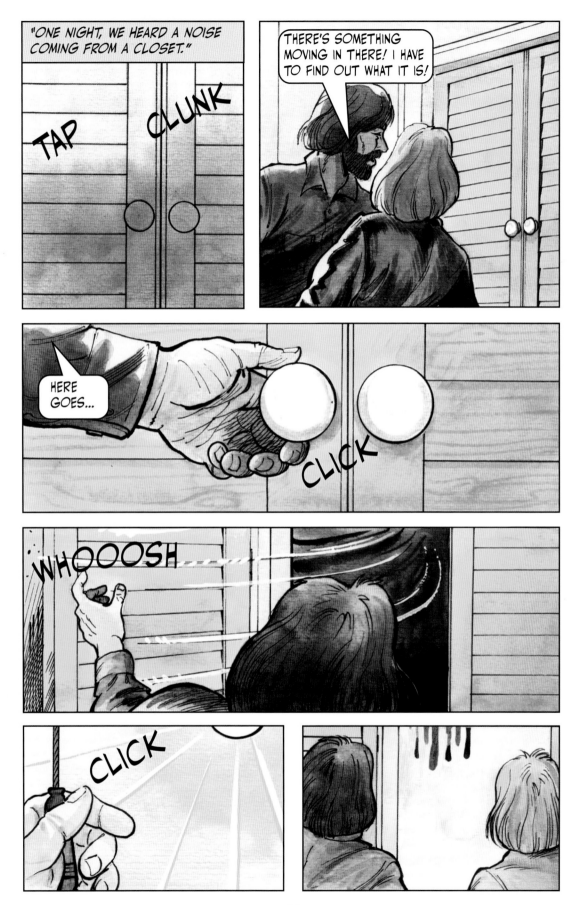

41

43

FACT OR FICTION?

Do ghosts really exist? Are they the returning spirits of the dead? Or are they just a trick of the light, projected by people's vivid imaginations?

FOR

Most cultures and religions believe in life after death. Therefore, a connection between the two worlds is only a small leap of faith. Very few people have seen ghosts, and we only have their word for it as "proof." Ghost hunter Andrew Green claims that you will never see a ghost if you look for it. However, some pictures have been taken of what appear to be ghostly figures. Even experts agree these are not fakes.

On September 19, 1936, Captain Provand and Indre Shira were taking photographs for a magazine at Raynham Hall, England. Shira saw something gliding down the stairs while Provand was focusing the camera. Shira fired the flashbulb, and the resulting photograph is shown here (left). Raynham Hall was said to be haunted by a ghost called the Brown Lady!

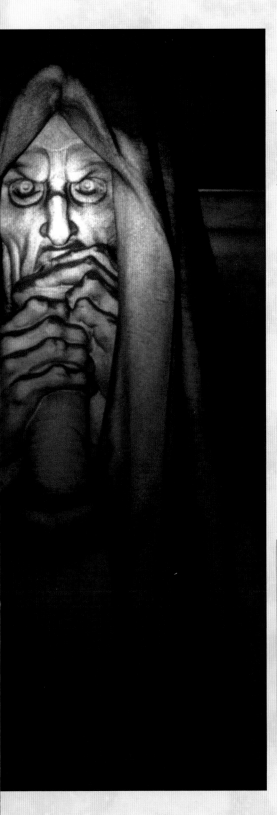

Scary otherworldly visions, like this statue in a Gothic church, continue to encourage our belief in ghosts and demons who cross over from the "other side."

AGAINST

In many cases, the events of a haunting or ghost sighting have been exaggerated and distorted. The truth of these reports is often quite ordinary. In 1869, photographer William Mumner was tried for selling photographs that he claimed included ghosts or spirits. In a hearing that attracted national interest, his photographs were thought to be created by darkroom techniques. All photographs of ghosts are open to charges of fraud, since the very nature of the developing process can allow for trickery, especially in today's world of computer-generated imagery.

Tricking audiences with ghostly visions at theaters in the Victorian era was easily done with the use of mirrors and glass.

GLOSSARY

afterlife The world that a person's spirit lives in after he or she has died.

ambassador Somebody employed by the government to represent his or her country in another country.

apparition Appearance of a ghost or other spiritual being.

buttress roots Roots that buckle up and are seen above the soil.

cloven When the foot of an animal is divided into two parts, such as a pig's hoof.

demonologist Someone who studies demons or evil spirits.

diplomatic The doing or saying of something in a way that does not upset or hurt others. Ambassadors are diplomats.

elevator A machine that carries people to different levels.

epic A very long poem that tells a complex story of adventure, that often features war and romance.

exorcism The banishment of evil spirits from inside a living body or a dwelling.

grisly Frightening and very horrible.

infest To swarm and spread over something; often refers to large groups of insects.

interference A blockage that prevents sound from being transferred. It is caused by two waves, such as sound waves, meeting each other.

intermediary A person who carries messages between two people.

lord A male who has power and authority over others, which has been passed down to him from a deceased, older family member.

ouija board A board covered with signs and letters of the alphabet used to send questions to, and receive answers from, the dead.

paranormal Something that cannot be explained.

poltergeist A ghost who is thought to create strange, loud noises.

psychic A person who has the ability to read minds.

séance A meeting in which a medium calls on spirits of the dead and passes messages between the dead and the living.

Shinnecock Indians A tribe of Native Americans that has lived for a very long time in eastern Long Island, New York.

underwriter Someone who is paid in small installments to insure a valuable object, such as a house. If the object is damaged or stolen, the underwriter pays to replace or repair it.

Victorian theater A type of dramatic performance that was popular in England during the reign of Queen Victoria. Ghosts were a popular subject of plays that were produced during this time.

welt A lump raised on the body by a blow.

FOR MORE INFORMATION

ORGANIZATIONS

American Ghost Society Headquarters
History & Hauntings Books Co.
515 East Third Street
Alton, IL 62002
http://www.prairieghosts.com/ags.html

International Society for Paranormal Research (ISPR)
4712 Admiralty Way, no. 541
Marina del Rey, CA 90292
http://www.ispr.net

FOR FURTHER READING

Chandler Warner, G. *The Ghost Town Mystery* (Boxcar Children's Mysteries). Morton Grove, IL: Albert Whitman & Company, 2002.

Claybourne, A., ed. *Poltergeists?: The Evidence and the Arguments* (Usbourne Paranormal Guides). Minneapolis, MA: Sagebrush, 1999.

Krovatin, C. *The Best Ghost Stories Ever.* New York: Scholastic, 2004.

Levy, J. *K.I.S.S. Guide to the Unexplained.* London, England: DK, 2002.

O'Neill, T., ed. *Ghosts and Poltergeists, Fact or Fiction?* Farmington Hills, MA: Greenhaven Press, 2002.

Vande Velde, V. *Companions of the Night.* New York: Magic Carpet Books, 2002.

Watkins, G. *Unsolved Mysteries Ghosts and Poltergeists.* New York: The Rosen Publishing Group, Inc., 2002.

INDEX

Web Sites

Due to the changing nature of Internet links, the Rosen Publishing Group, Inc., has developed an online list of Web sites related to the subject of this book. This site is updated regularly. Please use this link to access the list:

http://www.rosenlinks.com/grmy/ghpo